To the Library

Written by Rebecca Grazulis
Illustrated by Laura Merer
Cover illustrated by Mark Chambers

Louis Weber, C.E.O., Publications International, Ltd.
7373 North Cicero Avenue, Lincolnwood, Illinois 60712

Ground Floor, 59 Gloucester Place, London W1U 8JJ

Customer Service: 1-800-595-8484 or customer_service@pilbooks.com

www.pilbooks.com

Permission is never granted for commercial purposes.

p i kids is a registered trademark of Publications International, Ltd.

ISBN-13: 978-1-4127-9179-3
ISBN-10: 1-4127-9179-0

8 7 6 5 4 3 2 1

Hello! My name is Carol, and I'm a librarian.

Have you ever wanted to sail across the ocean, meet George Washington, or see what it would be like to be someone very different from who you are? You can do all of these things at my favorite place — the library.

There are lots of different parts of a library. This is the children's part. Lots of children just like you come here with their parents or friends when they are learning to read. Oh, the fun they have!

We even have story time. I love story time. Lots of children gather to listen to me read them a special story.

Grown-ups visit the library every day. Sometimes they want to read stories about made-up people and places. These stories are called fiction.

A story could be about outer space, an underwater city, or anything at all. If people tell me the kind of story they would like, I can help them find a book they would enjoy reading.

A student writing a history paper or a grown-up looking into vacation spots might come to the library. These people are in search of nonfiction. Written material about real people, places, and things is nonfiction.

If people know which book they are looking for, they can use a special computer to find where that book is in the library.

There are other things to read in a library in addition to books. Sometimes people are looking for an old newspaper. When newspapers get old, they are photographed and put on film similar to videotape. The film is wrapped around reels. Then the reels can be put on a special machine and read on a screen. This is called microfiche.

Do you know what a periodical is? It's just another name for a magazine! Periodicals can be about anything. Maybe some are delivered to your house. They can be about sports, medicine, movies, or anything at all.

A periodical is made up of different issues. Issues come out every week or month or maybe only once or twice a year.

There are many more things at the library than just reading materials. There are many ways to learn about the world, and you can find them at the library.

You can learn by watching movies. Music can also teach you a lot about other cultures. Another way to learn about the world is by using a computer.

When people leave the library, they can take a book home with them. They can check books out with a library card. A library card is your ticket to the world!